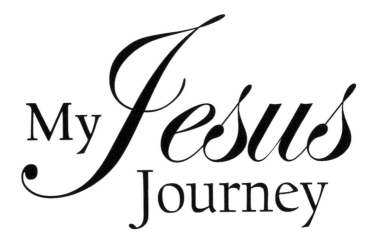

Spiritual Truths from the Desk
of Tim Barker

My Jesus Journey

Tim Barker, D. Min.

Superintendent of the South Texas
District of the Assemblies of God

Tim R. Barker Ministries

MY JESUS JOURNEY, Barker, Tim.
1st ed.

Formatting, proofing, and cover provided by:

Farley Dunn
of
Three Skillet Publishing

 THREE SKILLET

www.ThreeSkilletPublishing.com

Tim R. Barker Ministries

ISBN: 978-0-578-50310-3

Dedicated to
my parents,
Rev. Fred & Lucille Barker,
and my late brother,
Joe.

Preface

My heart has always been about doing the Lord's work and bringing the lost to Christ.

Many years ago, I worked the North Texas District's children's camps several summers while in college. I saw the spiritual need – even in children from church homes – and I was motivated to make the ministry my calling.

Today, I am privileged to serve in the offices of the South Texas District of the Assemblies of God, and my heart hasn't changed.

I want to be about the Lord's work. This book is another opportunity God has provided for me to share with you the conviction and burden for the lost Christ has laid upon my life.

Tim Barker, D. Min.
South Texas District Superintendent
Houston, Texas
May 2019

Acknowledgements

My wife, Jill, and my daughters, Jordin and Abby, are my strength through the valleys of life and my joy on the mountaintop. Their love and support have given me the courage to turn my musings on the good things of God into the very real substance of ink and paper.

My heartfelt thanks to Farley Dunn of Three Skillet Publishing for working tirelessly to get this book ready for the 67th Annual South Texas District Council convention. Farley donated his time and services to make this book happen, and I pray that God will reward his efforts and dedication to the cause of Christ.

My *Jesus* Journey

Blood Type

Matthew 26:28 (KJV)

For this is my blood of the new testament, which is shed for many for the remission of sins.

For Christmas a few years ago my family got me a DNA kit and I was amazed at the results of my lineage. My ancestry revealed much more than I'd been told by my parents and grandparents. DNA testifies to undeniable truths. My blood connected me to places and people I wouldn't have dreamed of.

Think about it . . . the same blood that flowed through Jesus' veins as a baby also pumped through His heart as He walked the shores of Galilee healing folks. When He hung on that wooden cross, the same blood ran from His veins, staining the cross and the linen that wrapped His body for burial. On the first resurrection day, that same blood-stained garment was proof of evidence that it was indeed Jesus who was risen.

As Andre Crouch wrote, "It still reaches to the highest mountain and it flows to the lowest valley. The blood that gives me strength from day to day will never lose its power." Jesus' blood is His gift of sacrifice that helps us understand unconditional love and the price of our salvation! It testifies that there is no distance God won't go to save each and every one of us.

Called

Philippians 4:13 (NKJV)

I can do all things through Christ who strengthens me.

We used to sing a song that said, "Rescue the perishing, duty demands it – strength for your labor the Lord will provide."

I often think of the sacrifice of our public servants, especially firefighters and police officers with their awesome sense of responsibility and duty. The sacrifice to their duty is apparent with every call they receive. The same should be true of those of us whose eternal life is secure in Jesus.

People are perishing all around us, whether physically, emotionally or most importantly, spiritually. We were created to be God's hands, feet and mouth while we have breath and life. I am grateful that He has provided the strength needed to accomplish such an enormous task. His Word declares in Philippians 4:13, "I can do all things through

Christ who strengthens me." Strength necessary to complete the assignment will be given once we respond in obedience.

So, activate your faith today, and extend hope to those who need rescue.

The Storm

Isaiah 25:4 (KJV)

For thou hast been a strength to the poor, a strength to the needy in his distress, a refuge from the storm . . .

Some time ago, devastating tornadoes destroyed parts of Alabama leaving behind 24 deaths with many people still missing. My heart breaks for all of them, but one family in particular lost 7 family members in one day. I cannot imagine the grief they're experiencing, and my prayers go out to them. Years ago, the movie *Twister* was released, and it portrayed a group of meteorologists chasing across the heartland as tornadoes devoured everything in their paths. I personally would find no thrill or enjoyment in that exercise. The thing that was obvious to me was even during raging winds there would often be moments of calm. That was because the storm chasers were in the eye of the storm.

Often we feel that the storms of our life are fierce and leave nothing but debris in their wake. But, because we know from where our protection comes – we can find and feel the shelter He provides. He is our safe place – our STORM SHELTER.

So, Let the Sun Shine In

1 John 4:12 (NIV)

No one has ever seen God; but if we love one another, God lives in us and his love is made complete in us.

When I was a kid we'd sing, "So, let the sun shine in, face it with a grin, smilers never lose and frowners never win . . ." Living down south, we are always eagerly awaiting colder weather because our summer heat is grueling. What we aren't prepared for is the gray & overcast skies. To cope, we travel to tropical climates and vacation somewhere more southern (and some visit their local tanning salons). None of this works to restore our need for sunshine. The first few days of spring warm us with sunny days, invigorating, revitalizing and refreshing us. Suddenly everything seems new again, because there's no substitute for the sun.

There is no substitute for Jesus either. Nothing or no one else will fill the void.

Christ's resurrection makes a way for us to be children of light. His love makes our joy and contentment possible, brightening even the harshest days with a hope that does not fade.

Just remember, because He shines within us, we are never without hope.

Devoted

Romans 12:10 (NIV)

Be devoted to one another in love. Honor one another above yourselves.

We used to sing lyrics of a song that said, "Holiness, holiness is what I long for . . . faithfulness, faithfulness is what You want from me."

The dictionary defines the word *devoted* as "dedicated, loyal, committed." These words are used often in our world because we're encouraged more and more to make time for "me" or #1!

However, God asks for something more permanent – FAITHFULNESS. Whether convenient or not, we're instructed in the Word to honor God and others. This will most likely require sacrifice, and maybe even postponing our own agenda. Yet, I am always amazed and inspired by a dedicated married partner, the surrender of a missionary, or the selfless love of a mother.

Devotion is more than the few minutes it takes to read a book or listen to our favorite worship chorus. "To devote" is a VERB which requires action. We live out our dedication to Christ each day when we put aside our own agenda and are faithful to God's will. I'm grateful for the example in Jesus Christ who modeled this for us and stands ready to help us whenever we call on His name.

Promises

Hebrews 10:23 (NIV)

Let us hold unswervingly to the hope we profess, for he who promised is faithful.

In the song *Thank You, Lord*, it says, *"For all that You've promised and all that You are, all that has carried me through."* When you think of the word "promise," you might also think of oath, guarantee, pledge, and/or vow. These are considered binding terms and are often used in legal documents, partnerships, and long-term commitments.

Both in Old Testament & New Testament Scriptures we find God's promises, which encourage faith in the believer's life. I am personally interested in the personalized promises God has for me. Well, it comes through study and obedience to the Word. For example, His Word speaks of assurance when we face trials and hardships; there is not a minute when He is not with you, there's confidence that He knows and He cares.

He will never leave or forsake us. Our concerns are His. God alone is able to see us through every problem. He has and forever will carry us through!

He Lives Forever

1 Corinthians 15:20-28 (NIV)

O But Christ has indeed been raised from the dead, the firstfruits of those who have fallen asleep. For since death came through a man, the resurrection of the dead comes also through a man. For as in Adam all die, so in Christ all will be made alive. But each in turn: Christ, the firstfruits; then, when he comes, those who belong to him. Then the end will come, when he hands over the kingdom to God the Father after he has destroyed all dominion, authority and power. For he must reign until he has put all his enemies under his feet. The last enemy to be destroyed is death. For he "has put everything under his feet." Now when it says that "everything" has been put under him, it is clear that this does not include God himself, who put everything under Christ. When he has done this,

then the Son himself will be made subject
to him who put everything under him, so
that God may be all in all.

I remember the Easter Sunday morning I
entered into our resurrection Sunday celebration
and our music director had scheduled a tuba
ensemble. Their music filled our auditorium
with the glorious sounds of the season, with
"He arose a victor from the dark domain, and he
lives forever with his saints to reign." I assure
you, it was a majestic experience and something
I'll cherish forever. Not only was the music
transforming but the truth of scripture envel-
oped me.

We've all lost someone in death who was
special to us. Some of them had long life
while others left us at a young age. Either
way, we've felt the intensity of grief, leaving
us feeling cold and lonely. Death is inevi-
table. Still the details surrounding death hold
a great mystery, which makes us often afraid
and uncertain.

Jesus conquered death and overcame it
forever. The Lord of life was dead and buried
but rose victorious. So, there is no need for
fear! The victory is won when we trust in our
living Savior. Again, He rose a victor from
the dark domain, and He lives forever with

His saints to reign. Because He lives, I live and I can face the uncertainties!

Victory Is Mine

1 John 5:4 (KJV)

*For whatsoever is born of God overcometh
the world: and this is the victory that
overcometh the world, even our faith.*

A photo renown in U.S. history was taken
on August 14, 1945. The photo is titled, "V-J
Day in Times Square," capturing a young sailor
who just return from war, kissing a nurse in a
moment of excitement. The background is filled
with folks celebrating the fact that the Japanese
have surrendered and World War II has ended.

There is obvious celebration in those
moments of victory involving a nation or
country. But as followers of Christ, we don't
have to wait for such occasions to be happy.
We have joy available each day because God
has made us victorious over all things –
including sin and death.

It's a new day in the Lord. Spread His
Word and CELEBRATE! Victory is YOURS!
The battle has already been won!

There's At Least One in the Crowd

Nehemiah 4:7-9 (NKJV)

*Now it happened, when Saballat, Tobiah,
the Arabs, the Ammonites, and the
Ashdodites heard that the walls of
Jerusalem were being restored and the
gaps were beginning to be closed, that they
became very angry, and all of them
conspired together to come and attack
Jerusalem and create confusion.
Nevertheless we made our prayer to our
God, and because of them we set a watch
against them day and night.*

Nehemiah had to deal with the same type
of folks that we deal with today: distractors
who torment and do everything within their
power to interfere with work. We often call
them "arm-chair quarterbacks," but they're
much more than that. For example, Saballat
first tried to stop the work by mocking and

ridiculing the Jews. When that didn't work, he changed his tactics to fear, entrapment, and political maneuvering. The contrast between Nehemiah and Sanballat was worlds apart. Nehemiah's leadership and character dealt with every assault of Sanballat and despite it, his godly vision was completed.

It's easy to sit on the sideline and complain or offer suggestions, but until you are in the lead you don't have a clue. Our American political landscape is filled with those who know better than the one called to occupy the White House. Until they sit in the chair, they ought to guard their opinions.

Several lessons can be learned from studying Sanballat's assaults, threats, and schemes.

- Expect distractors.
- Don't give them the time of day (easier said than done!).
- Trust God to protect you and your reputation.
- Keep your hands to the plow and don't look back.
- And, keep your weapon in one hand and your tool in another.

Grounded

Psalm 68:32-35 (KJV)

*Sing unto God, ye kingdoms of the earth; O
sing praises unto the Lord; Selah: To him that
rideth upon the heavens of heavens, which
were of old; lo, he doth send out his voice,
and that a mighty voice. Ascribe ye strength
unto God: his excellency is over Israel, and
his strength is in the clouds. O God, thou art
terrible out of thy holy places: the God of
Israel is he that giveth strength and power
unto his people. Blessed be God.*

We often sing, "We bow down and worship
Him now; How great, how awesome is He."
This is more than lyrics to a chorus; it's a
character trait which expresses humility. It
implies that we come powerless and let go of
our own aspirations. There's no more significant act of humility than to empty yourself and give total allegiance to another. And,
no one is more worthy than our awesome

Lord, the Creator of all the Universe. He is our Savior, Author and the Finisher of our Faith. When Jesus left His throne for us, He sacrificed all power for death on the cross.

We honor our God by embracing gratitude for Him who, in His holiness, held mankind responsible for sin, while providing a way to forgiveness. Our Almighty God is capable of awesome grace and power! So, when we sing HOLY IS THE LORD, we express as the Psalmist, "Father, I humbly repent of not always giving You the respect You so rightfully deserve."

For Real?

Romans 8:26-27 (NIV)

*In the same way, the Spirit helps us in our
weakness. We do not know what we ought to
pray for, but the Spirit himself intercedes
for us through wordless groans. And he who
searches our hearts knows the mind of the
Spirit, because the Spirit intercedes for
God's people in accordance with the will of
God.*

We all occasionally need a reality check!
I've often prayed for patience, only to find
myself in the slowest checkout line at the
grocery store or stuck in bumper-to-bumper
traffic. I think God sometimes gives us
opportunity to practice what we pray. He is
actually answering our prayers, but not like
we had hoped or anticipated.

When we pray, our approach is to ask for
what we think we need, but do we really
know what we are asking or what we even

need? When prayers go unanswered or we get a different response, we ask, is God really listening? Are my prayers even getting through? Thank God for the Holy Spirit who knows the Father's heart, who knows how to reconcile the two so that we ultimately receive God's best and not everything we ask for.

Holy Spirit, thank you for seeing the good and perfect will of God completed in me.

Sheltered from the Storm

Matthew 14:30 (KJV)

But when he saw the wind boisterous, he was afraid; and beginning to sink, he cried, saying, Lord, save me.

One of my all-time favorite songs says, "The raging storms may 'round us beat ... we'll never leave our safe retreat. He's our shelter in the time of storm."

Biblical personalities like Joseph, Daniel, Ruth and others seem like GIANTS OF FAITH when we read of the trials they faced and how they responded. On the other hand, Peter's struggle we often relate to. He experienced fear, anger, doubt and faith.

For example, in Matthew 14:30, Peter was consumed with fear, crying out to Jesus to save him as the wind and the waves were about to overtake him.

I can relate to Peter's feelings, because I've left some storms behind, been in the middle of many storms or saw some fierce storm approaching that was beyond my control.

So, if you're treading water today or maybe feel like you're about to go under the water in some area of your life – stretch out your hand and cry to God to save you. Jesus cares and has the ability to lift you up, providing a safe retreat from whatever storm you may find yourself in. I pray that you'll put your hand in the hand of the Man who stills the water.

Wake Up

Lamentations 3:22-23 (NIV)

Because of the Lord's great love we are not consumed, for his compassions never fail. They are new every morning; great is your faithfulness.

In 1977 I was 16 years old and remember learning a song which we would sing on Youth Group trips.

The lyrics were, "Jesus' love is bubbling over, bubbling over in my soul." We'd also add to our repertoire the song, "Jesus is the Rock and He rolls my blues away." Those were more than just youthful chants; they've become reality. At 56 years old, if only I could wake up and roll out of bed each morning with a winning mindset. After all, we are living and breathing with purpose. God watches over us in sleep and protects us from harm because He has a future for us beyond anything we can believe.

We are living testimonies of God's

strength each and every day that we breathe air. He doesn't just provide us a new day, but new mercies accompany the rising sun. So, whatever circumstances surround you, God's love is greater. He provides the necessary strength to endure and to win over today's challenges, because He is with us. The fact that you woke up today is proof.

Family Bonds

2 Corinthians 4:17 (NIV)

For our light and momentary troubles are achieving for us an eternal glory that far outweighs them all.

Recently my family experienced back to back losses, when my sister-in-law, Bobbie, graduated to her eternal home, winning her battle over the terrible disease, Alzheimer's. A year later, my oldest brother, Joe, went home. He had expressed his weariness from the struggles of illness and loss of his wife of 63 years and longed to be home. Our entire family was affected not only because of the losses, but because of the pain we saw our loved ones experience. We never doubted our family's bond during these tough times, rather the connection was strengthened through our adversities. Today, I value my family more than ever and cherish the times we have together, not taking them for granted.

The family of God should respond to each other the same way. Grief and hardships will come because no one is immune. Christ Jesus, Himself, even suffered, but He overcame. That provides hope in difficult times of despair.

Realize that trials and pain will come. And when they do, we need each other like never before. We can provide hope as a part of the family. I'm grateful for my biological family and for my family in Christ, because God is at the head – our protector and provider. He sustains us through our momentary afflictions and difficulties.

What's Your Story?

Mark 16:15 (KJV)

And he said unto them, Go ye into all the world, and preach the gospel to every creature.

One of my favorite radio personalities was Paul Harvey, best known for his statement, "Now for the rest of the story . . ." If I didn't hear anything else he shared, I perked up for the real scoop.

We often listen to friends who share detailed accounts of events concerning their lives, while anticipating a positive conclusion. Sometimes, however, that's not always the case and the ending isn't what we'd hoped for. I'm grateful that there is always more to the story because Jesus came and brought us peace and redemption when we couldn't find it for ourselves. We have "the rest of the story" to offer to our friends who feel hopeless and helpless, because our powerful ending is the best and nothing compares.

So, from the words of one of my all-time favorite hymns, *"I love to tell the story because I know 'tis true; it satisfies my longings as nothing else can do."*

Hide and Seek

Matthew 11:28 (NIV)

*Come to me, all you who are weary and
burdened, and I will give you rest.*

I loved playing Hide & Seek as a kid and it
surprises me that my grandkids also enjoy it.

My friend & legendary song writer, Lanny
Wolfe, wrote the song *Seeking For Me* with
powerful lyrics that say, "From the splendor
of heaven to the world down below. From a
manger to an old rugged tree. From the dawn
of creation through the corridors of time, the
Savior in love was seeking for me." Why
would Jesus go seeking after us when we
separated ourselves from Him? It's because
we were created to a part of His family. Our
sin is what separated us from Him and caused
us to seek a place to hide. I'm grateful that
Jesus came seeking for me.

Lanny's song says, "He was reaching for
me but I resisted His touch. Instead I reached
for other things I thought meant so much.

Things of value in earth's market, I had sought all of them. But, all the time I was seeking, I was seeking for Him.

"So, I reached out to Jesus, crying, Lord, hear my plea, for I want You to take all of me. Then out of darkness I saw His light giving me a brand-new start. Oh, praise the Lord, Jesus found me when I gave Him all my heart."

I'm so glad I've been found! How about you? Are you still HIDING from Him?

We Have a Firm Foundation

Psalm 61:2 (NLT)

From the ends of the earth I call to you, I call as my heart grows faint; lead me to the rock that is higher than I.

Lyrics from one of the greatest hymns ever written say, "Could my tears forever flow, could my zeal no longer know, these for sin could not atone – Thou must save and Thou alone."

Something known to be "rock solid" can withstand immense pressure. In Matthew's Gospel, chapter 7:24-27 it reads, *"Therefore everyone who hears these words of mine and puts them into practice is like a wise man who built his house on the rock. The rain came down, the streams rose, and the winds blew and beat against that house; yet it did not fall, because it had its foundation on the rock. But everyone who hears these words of mine and does not put them into practice is like a foolish man who built his house on sand. The rain came down, the streams rose, and the winds blew and beat against that house, and it fell with a great crash."* As believers, our lives are built upon the ROCK or foundation of Jesus.

As the church, we are built on the same foundation and the enemy cannot destroy it. So, who or what are we to fear? We can take refuge – we can hide behind the Rock and rest within the security He provides.

Even when life gets crazy and things are unsettled and unsure, we don't cling to such. We establish our footing upon the Rock of Ages – the Rock that is higher and stronger and surer than we are.

Psalm 61:2 says, *"From the ends of the earth I call to you, I call as my heart grows faint; lead me to the rock that is higher than I."*

Morning Is Coming

Matthew 28:19 (NLT)

Therefore go and make disciples of all nations, baptizing them in the name of the Father and of the Son and of the Holy Spirit.

Most of the time when we are witnessing to an unbeliever who doesn't know Christ, we introduce them to the Book of Romans.

We explain that the result of our sinfulness is eternal separation from God – ultimate death. In that same passage, however, is the promise of eternal life.

Jesus became victorious over sin and the grave, and we no longer have to live in fear or even grieve death. Rather, we enjoy and celebrate the salvation that Jesus provided us by His own sacrifice. The truth is that we will all one day face physical death, but His sacrifice changes everything regarding our perspective of it.

Death no longer has the final say. Because

of Jesus Christ, there is life!

Matthew 28:19 says, *"Therefore go and make disciples of all nations, baptizing them in the name of the Father and of the Son and of the Holy Spirit."*

We used to sing with such fervency, "EVERYBODY OUGHT TO KNOW WHO JESUS IS," and it rings even more true today in my heart! EVERYBODY deserves to know!

Feet to Your Faith

John 20:21 (NIV)

Again Jesus said, "Peace be with you! As the Father has sent me, I am sending you."

Too many Christians seem to be unfamiliar with the Great Commission and the command to spread the Gospel and make disciples. We forget that we were saved with someone else in mind. Some think that evangelism is the professional's job. Not so! Jesus' charge was to all believers to continue the work of kingdom-building. He didn't simply make a suggestion, rather a divine order! We are duty-bound to take the Good News outward, to bring comfort and hope to a desperate humanity. If we don't – then who will?

Today is the day to put feet to our faith. We've been given a heavenly directive to show love and concern. Pray with me . . . "Lord, show me how to serve people and love those you cherish."

God Will Take Care of You

Isaiah 46:3-4 (NIV)

Listen to me, you descendants of Jacob, all the remnant of the people of Israel, you whom I have upheld since your birth, and have carried since you were born. Even to your old age and gray hairs I am he, I am he who will sustain you. I have made you and I will carry you; I will sustain you and I will rescue you.

"Be not dismayed whate'er betide . . . no matter what may be the test, God will take care of you."

Throughout every stage of life God promises to be with us. This means that no matter what we face, we can be assured God's not surprised. Critical illness or terminal diagnosis may become our fate, yet God is still in control.

God's word reminds us that He not only goes before us, but He journeys along with us and His goodness and mercy are following after us. I assure you if you're in one of those long nights, be reminded that JOY COMES IN THE MORNING.

Jesus Loves Me

Proverbs 8:17 (NIV)

I love those who love me, and those who seek me find me.

"Jesus loves me, this I know, for the Bible tells me so . . ." As simple as these familiar words are, they speak volumes to me of Christ's love and devotion. The message of the Gospel is really just that simple . . . "Yes, Jesus loves me."

Throughout the Word of God, you find God's unconditional love: "Who shall separate us from the love of Christ?" (Romans 8:35). "We love Him because He first loved us." (1 John 4:19). "For God so loved the world that He gave . . ." (John 3:16). In those times that you feel unlovable or unworthy of love, take captive your thoughts and replace them with the truth of God's Word . . . "Yes, Jesus loves me."

My How Time Flies

Psalm 46:10 (NIV)

*He says, "Be still, and know that I am God;
I will be exalted among the nations, I will
be exalted in the earth."*

I remember when I was a kid, I thought I'd never grow up. If I could just finally reach the ripe age of eighteen, everything would fall into place, so I thought. Now, as an adult with mortgage payments, children and grandchildren, career demands, and aging family member challenges, I find myself wondering where time has gone.

Instead of wishing your life away, savor the moments of today. Take time to appreciate what God has done and is still doing. Whether the challenges you're facing today are financial, rebellious children or difficult colleagues, everything is designed to demonstrate God's love and mercy.

Time moves so quickly, but God has given us the gift of eternal life TODAY! And, to

add to it – ETERNITY IS STILL PROM-
ISED! So, be still, and trust that God is in
control of every detail that controls your life.

Take a moment to reflect on the lyrics of a
powerful song recorded by CeCe Winans,
titled, TOMORROW . . .

Jesus said,
"Here I stand, won't you please let me in?"
And you said,
"I will tomorrow."

Jesus said,
"I am he who supplies all your needs,"
And you said,
"I know, but tomorrow, ooh, tomorrow, I'll give
my life
tomorrow, I thought about today, but it's so much
easier to say . . ."

Tomorrow, who promised you tomorrow?
Better choose the Lord today, for
tomorrow very well might be too late.

Jesus said,
"Here I stand, won't you please take my hand?"
And you said,
"I will tomorrow."

Jesus said,
"I am he who supplies all your needs,"

And you said,
"I know, but tomorrow, ooh, tomorrow, I'll give
my life
tomorrow. I thought about today, oooohh,
but it's so much easier to say . . ."

Tomorrow, who promised you tomorrow?
Better choose the Lord today, for
tomorrow very well might be too late.

And who said tomorrow would ever come for
you?
Still you laugh and play and continue to say,
"Tomorrow."
Forget about tomorrow, won't you give
your life today, oohh.
Please don't just turn and walk away.
Tomorrow, tomorrow is not promised.
Don't let this moment slip away.
Your tomorrow could very well begin today.

He'll Be Back

Matthew 21:9 (KJV)

*And the multitudes that went before, and
that followed, cried, saying, Hosanna to the
son of David: Blessed is he that cometh in
the name of the Lord; Hosanna in the
highest.*

1. I am watching for the coming of the glad
   millennial day,
   When our blessed Lord shall come and catch
   His waiting bride away.
   Oh! my heart is filled with rapture as I labor,
   watch, and pray,
   For our Lord is coming back to earth again.
   Refrain
   > Oh, our Lord is coming back to earth
   > again.
   > Yes, our Lord is coming back to earth
   > again.
   > Satan will be bound a thousand years;
   > we'll have no tempter then,

After Jesus shall come back to earth
again.
2. Jesus' coming back will be the answer to
earth's sorrowing cry,
For the knowledge of the Lord shall fill
the earth and sea and sky.
God shall take away all sickness and the
sufferer's tears will dry,
When our Savior will come back to earth
again. [Refrain]
3. Yes, the ransomed of the Lord shall come
to Zion then with joy,
And in all His holy mountain nothing
hurts or shall destroy.
Perfect peace shall reign in every heart,
and love without alloy,
After Jesus shall come back to earth
again. [Refrain]
4. Then the sin and sorrow, pain and death
of this dark world shall cease,
In a glorious reign with Jesus of a
thousand years of peace.
All the earth is groaning, crying for that
day of sweet release,
For our Jesus shall come back to earth
again. [Refrain]

I intended to share the first verse, but, I
got carried away as I read the lyrics and

wanted to share them all. From Matthew 21:9, we read, "Hosanna to the Son of David! Blessed is He who comes in the name of the Lord!"

One day, very soon, Jesus is coming to take His people home. He came the first time in the person of Jesus. The people of Jerusalem knew a King was among them when Jesus entered riding on a donkey.

The Lord will come again, and don't forget that He already knows the date and hour. At that moment His Son will win the final victory. Until that time, we are urged to be watchful and always ready.

Until that day He returns, we must keep living our lives, caring for our opportunities, using the gifts we've been given to serve Him. But, keep an eye toward the sky, because HE IS COMING SOON!

Celebrate

1 Thessalonians 4:17 (KJV)

Then we which are alive and remain shall be caught up together with them in the clouds, to meet the Lord in the air: and so shall we ever be with the Lord.

One of my favorite hymns of all times says, *"When clothed in His brightness transported I rise to meet Him in clouds of the sky, His perfect salvation, His wonderful love, I'll shout with the millions on high."*

I am constantly planning events for our district ministries and often ask our team for an update on the registration. What I want to know is, are people as excited about this event as I am? Have they registered or are they procrastinating?

Can you imagine the preparations going on in heaven as Jesus plans for the group that will be joining Him for His wedding feast? I wonder if He asks, "How many have RSVP'd today?" Are you prepared with the robes of righteousness He's provided?

There's a place at the table with your name on it and He's taken care of all the arrangements. I sure hope you've said YES, because one day soon – the CELEBRATIONS WILL BEGIN!

Ministering Spirits

Hebrews 1:14 (KJV)

Are they not all ministering spirits, sent forth to minister for them who shall be heirs of salvation?

I was driving on one of our Houston Interstates one day and a car came out of what appeared to be nowhere and I had to slam on my brakes to avoid a collision. My car went into an immediate fishtail.

I thought for sure I was going to hit multiple vehicles, sending many innocent people to area hospitals. In that instant of trying to make corrections and steer my truck back into control, I yelled out a prayer for God to help! Within seconds my truck was on the shoulder, right up against a concrete median, facing the opposite direction from traffic. I was stopped almost immediately after praying. There was not a scratch on my car or any others.

Suppose God used angels to spare my life

that day? Perhaps He sent them to take control of my steering wheel. Hebrews 1:14 tells us that angels are ministering spirits. They are the extension of God on earth, assisting us in our time of need. They are attentive to the prayers we express, ready to help at God's command. I'm grateful, living in the nation's 4th largest city and traveling the roadways, that God has angels all around to keep and protect me – on call at a moment's notice.

When we sing my friend, Geron Davis' song, *Holy Ground*, it sure makes the lyrics, "and I know that there are angels all around," mean so much more.

Sing

Psalm 150:1 (KJV)

Praise ye the LORD. Praise God in his sanctuary: praise him in the firmament of his power.

From the classic hymn, *We're Marching to Zion*, are these powerful lyrics... *"Then let our songs abound and every tear be dry. We're marching through Immanuel's ground to fairer worlds on high."*

Worship has been a part of every century as a natural expression of praise. Even when they're not certain to whom the focus is on, nevertheless, there's an instinct within everyone to express appreciation.

The Psalms records songs written in praise & adoration. Later, hymns became our passionate articulation of beliefs. There are times rhythm guitars lead us into a folksier demonstration, or there's one of my favorites - the sound of hundred-voice choirs in a cathedral. Regardless, the familiarity of the lyrics or music, our souls are lifted in worship.

Having visited various nations over my lifetime, music brings everyone together in true worship to God. Musical styles will change, but one thing remains – PRAISE & GLORY TO GOD will last throughout all eternity.

So, let our songs continue. Raise your voice and SING!

Heir

Micah 5:2 (NIV)

But you, Bethlehem Ephrathah, though you are small among the clans of Judah, out of you will come for me one who will be ruler over Israel, whose origins are from of old, from ancient times.

A particular lyric from the Christmas carol, *O Little Town of Bethlehem*, that is rarely utilized says, "No ear may hear His coming, but in this world of sin, where meek souls will receive Him still, the dear Christ enters in." In classic literature, hidden identity is popular. The surprise comes when the least likely person becomes heir to the kingdom. It almost sounds like a Hallmark movie with a twist.

Jesus Christ, the Prince of Peace and the heir to God's kingdom, never hid His identity, still many in our world have never recognized Him. From the beginning, the folks in Bethlehem didn't acknowledge His coming, because He was born in humility – in a stable. I'm grateful that even when we, like the people in Bethlehem, fail to recognize His presence, He still extends compassion to us, always standing at the door of our hearts, just waiting for an invitation in. Why don't you invite Jesus into your world today!

Bad to Blessing

Psalm 20:1 (NIV)

May the Lord answer you when you are in distress; may the name of the God of Jacob protect you.

In the song *Day by Day*, these lyrics were written . . . "Help me then in every tribulation, so to trust Thy promise, O Lord."

Bad days are the worst and no one is exempt. Have you ever considered that your bad day might just be a blessing? We've all been running late to work, only to find traffic is backed up all because of a car accident. Think about it . . . had you been on time, that might have been you and your car.

Life throws us unexpected circumstances that seem poorly timed and so inconvenient. Yet what we don't see are the "almost" events that God has shielded us from.

The Bible doesn't say "if" trouble comes; it says "when" trouble comes. So, while troubles are guaranteed, be thankful: God is able to use even the bad days to bless you. Trust Him in it, even if you can't see the blessing beyond the difficulty.

Lord, help me look for today's blessings in disguise!

Worthy

Psalm 107:22 (NIV)

*Let them sacrifice thank offerings and
tell of his works with songs of joy.*

There are all kinds of celebrity award
shows each year. Hollywood presents its lifetime achievement awards to folks who, over
decades, have received significant acclaim for
their work. During the ceremony, clips from
their movies are shown. I've often imagined a
similar setting where the one true God is on
display for all He's done. Throughout history
– and certainly in my own life, He has put His
holiness, and love, and goodness, and justice,
might and grace on display. From Eve to
Daniel, from Mary to the boy with the loaves
and fishes – God has shown Himself worthy
of our acclaim.

But, just think about it – HE'S NOT
DONE YET! He still continues to accomplish
His purpose in us.

So, this Thanksgiving, I encourage you to

look to the future with great expectation –
God is there before you, preparing the way!

Family

Matthew 18:4 (NLT)

So anyone who becomes as humble as this little child is the greatest in the Kingdom of Heaven.

A popular sitcom when I was a kid was titled *All In The Family* and we watched it often. I never felt that it was the most valuable to my upbringing because it seemed to be contrary to everything I was taught about family. Archie was loud, boisterous and quite cantankerous at times, especially in dealing with his children, Gloria & Michael. He also didn't contribute much to his wife, Edith's self-esteem. My dad, Fred, was a much better example for me to follow. I was usually referred to as "son," which for me carried a high regard. I was blessed with amazing, loving and caring parents, who I never doubted their commitment. They were both there when I humbled myself in repentance at the age of twelve and I was reborn into God's family, becoming His child (son).

I've found that as my Heavenly Father, He loves me no matter what. I also realize one of the greatest benefits of being adopted into His family is my joint inheritance with my elder brother, Jesus. He is now my Savior and brother. Isn't that cool?

My place in the family isn't based on what I can do, how much I have, or how many people I know. It comes from a simple, yet powerful act, of kneeling in repentance and acknowledging my need for mercy & grace. In that humility – I found true status – as His beloved child.

Prayer

Luke 11:2 (NLT)

Jesus [told His disciples], "THIS IS HOW YOU SHOULD PRAY . . ."

Prayer isn't a big mystery. It's a matter of talking, and then listening; telling God what we're thinking, and then seeking His thoughts; sharing what we need, and then asking Him what's best.

Prayer is the language of our relationship. The better we know Him, the easier the conversation flows. I talk with Him as I talk with a friend. Another step in the process involves Scripture, which reveals to us His character. He's a loving Father and Scripture reveals that His shoulders are strong enough that I can lean on Him. The Word describes Him as forgiving, therefore He wants to help in our times of crisis. It is revealed in the Bible that He's understanding and constantly building our character . . . and, He is just and often times must deal with the wrongs of the world.

Take the chance to talk to Him today. He is listening!

Come and Dine

Matthew 22:3 (NIV)

He sent his servants to those who had been invited to the banquet to tell them to come, but they refused to come.

In the 1970s a popular chorus was *His Banner Over Me Is Love*, and one verse said, "I'm feasting at His banqueting table; His banner over Me is love." We would often sing another hymn that said, "Jesus has a table spread where the saints of God are fed; He invites His chosen people . . . COME & DINE!"

Jesus has prepared a CONTINUAL PARTY, even sending out invitations, yet many have declined. Not only did the angels in heaven rejoice when we accepted the Father's invitation, but there's the promise of life more abundantly that He's given. The party I'm speaking of will be unlike any other celebration that anyone's ever seen. Jesus, Himself, will be the host, and at this time we will rejoice together that sin and death have been defeated.

Invitations are still going out each time we proclaim the Gospel message! Let's intensify our efforts because the table's being prepared for the glorious celebration. I believe the caterers are almost done and the party is about to begin!

Well Done

Matthew 25:21 (NLT)

The master was full of praise. "Well done, my good and faithful servant. You have been faithful in handling this small amount, so now I will give you many more responsibilities. Let's celebrate together!"

It is when we realize that God has given us exactly what we need in order to accomplish His Kingdom work – time, abilities and resources – that we are successful & content in ministry. So, don't get caught up in the comparison game against neighbors, friends or even family members, because what's important is that we have HIM! He is the One who supplies, supports and multiplies our efforts. We must also realize that not only are we supported, but no one else has been given our portion or part.

As we care for what God has entrusted to us we have to keep in mind that He delights in helping us accomplish HIS WORK. And, when we finally finish our tasks, we too will hear Him say, "WELL DONE." Imagine that celebration!

My prayer is: Dear Jesus, help me to use the resources I have wisely and for your glory! NOT MINE!

Persistence, Part A

Nehemiah 4:15 (KJV)

And it happened, when our enemies heard that it was known to us, and that God had brought their plot to nothing, that all of us returned to the wall, everyone to his work.

It's been said that one of the greatest tests of leadership is how you handle opposition. Trust me, if you're a leader, you will encounter opposition. When I go for long periods of time without opposition, I begin to worry why. And, it's not the opposition that seems to trip me up as much as where and from whom the opposition occasionally comes, like people you actually trusted.

Well, Nehemiah modeled the right response:

- Rely totally on God.
- Respect the opposition (this is hard to do).

- Reinforce your weak points (first admit and identify them).
- Reassure the people (sheep get weary at times when there's silence in the storms).
- Refuse to quit (help me on this one, Lord).
- Renew the people's strength continually.

Much like some of us, Nehemiah had to deal with problems from the outside (people who didn't have a vested interest in anything he was doing). He dealt with ridicule, resistance and rumor. Does any of that sound familiar? Nehemiah also dealt with disputes about food, property, and taxes (and I get the tax argument).

So, what can be learned from this faithful and courageous leader? PERSISTENCE is the ultimate gauge of our leadership. I'm not about to say it's an easy task, but the secret is to outlast our critics. WE MUST stay committed to God and to His ultimate calling!

I've Fallen and I Must Get Back Up

Persistence, Part B

Judges 3:7-9 (NKJV)

So the children of Israel did evil in the sight of the Lord. They forgot the Lord their God . . . Therefore the anger of the Lord was hot against Israel and He sold them into the hand of Cushan-Rishathaim king of Mesopotamia, and the children of Israel served Cushan-Rishathaim eight years. When the children of Israel cried out to the Lord, the Lord raised up a deliverer from the children of Israel, who delivered them.

Austin O'Malley said, "The fact that you have been knocked down is interesting, but the length of time you stay down is important."

In life you will have problems! Trust me! Are you going to give up and stay down, settling for defeat or get back up? If you fall, get up and recognize what caused you to fall, learn from it, and get back to business.

Henry Ford said, "Failure is the opportunity to begin again more intelligently." His words make me think of the lyrics to a song we sang years ago, "Just when things look hopeless, He reaches out His hand because God delivers again!" TAKE HIS HAND in your hand and let Him lead! Stay in sync with Him and continue the journey until it's complete!

Inside First Before Outside

Numbers 32:13 (NKJV)

So the Lord's anger was aroused against Israel, and He made them wander in the wilderness forty years, until all the generations that had done evil in the sight of the Lord was gone.

The first person you'll ever lead is you! You can't lead without disciplining yourself. If the Israelites had remembered this, they wouldn't have wandered aimlessly for 40 years in the desert. The reason they didn't get to the Promised Land was not because they missed their turns and got lost. They didn't get to the Promised Land because they hadn't prepared to go in the first place.

So, this causes us to pause and ask the question - are we ready? How do we measure up in the area of self-discipline? It was Plato that said, "The first and the last victory is to conquer oneself."

If we plan to lead as God has called us to lead, we must practice self-discipline:

1. Develop and follow our priorities.
2. Make our goal a disciplined lifestyle.
3. Challenge our excuses.
4. Remove the idea of rewards until the job is finished.
5. Stay focused on results.

I'll leave you with this one thought . . .

NEVER TRADE WHAT YOU WANT AT THE MOMENT FOR WHAT YOU WANT MOST!

Inner Circle

1 Samuel 22:1-2 (NKJV)

When his brothers and all his father's house heard it, they went down there to him. And everyone who was in debt, and everyone who was discontented gathered to him. SO he became captain over them.

You might consider my using the passage to illustrate this point a real stretch. But, I believe what made David a great leader, besides the fact that he was a man after God's own heart, was those he surrounded himself with.

David was surrounded by quality people (true friends) way before he became a great leader. And, his followers would not have made anyone's top ten of most influential people. Some of them were misfits. Under David's leadership his team was transformed into a winning team. As David grew in his leadership skills, stronger people surrounded him.

He was an awesome leader and a team builder, yet just like us – he was anything but perfect. He was flawed and failed, yet God chose to use him for His glory. I'm convinced that it was partially because of his inner circle that he became the great man we know him to be.

Be careful with those you surround yourself with. In my experience (sadly to say) some I allowed closest to me attacked me and ultimately abandoned me. Very few remained but they've proven themselves and to them I owe a great deal of gratitude. I wouldn't have made it without them!

No Fun Removing

1 Timothy 3:1 (TMB)

If anyone wants to provide leadership in the church, good! But there are preconditions.

The best way (actually the only way) to empower people is to evaluate them. By giving inexperienced people too much authority you are setting them up for failure. The same can be true of people with lots of experience. If you move too slowly, they'll become frustrated and you run the risk of losing them (and their giftings).

In 1898, Albert Einstein applied to Munich Technical Institute for admission and was rejected. They said, "He will never amount to much." Instead of school, he worked as an inspector at the Swiss Patent Office and during his free time refined the theory of relativity.

As leaders, we must believe that everyone has the potential to succeed. It is our job to help develop their potential. Consider these three areas regarding those you're attempting to promote:

1. Knowledge - Think about what people need to know in order to do anything you intend to give them.
2. Skill - Nothing is more frustrating than being asked to do something for which you have no ability.
3. Desire - no amount of skill, knowledge, or potential can help a person succeed if he doesn't have the desire to be successful.

It's easier to PROMOTE than to DEMOTE! Be careful because people's feelings and your reputation are at stake!

Gaining Knowledge

Proverbs 1:7 (KJV)

The fear of the Lord is the beginning of knowledge, but fools despise wisdom and instruction.

In times of decision, wisdom can be a leader's best friend. I've sat in meetings when we circled the wagons a dozen times and never found the necessary conclusion. The person in the room who will walk away with the greatest amount of influence will be the one with the wisdom to draw a conclusion that not only works, but receives the blessing of the others.

What a beautiful picture is depicted for us in Proverbs 1 of wisdom - a woman crying out in the streets. Wisdom doesn't hide herself - but - she shouts publicly! We can learn from this.

The Ultimate Reunion

Matthew 24:42 (NLT)

Therefore keep watch, because you do not know on what day your Lord will come.

I must admit that I'm a sucker for all the surprise military reunions where loved ones are reunited with those who are serving our country. I usually cry like a baby and joy fills my heart each time I view one of these. Some folks wait months or even years to see their loved one. I also enjoy the programs where folks are introduced to loved ones whom they were separated from all of their lives, or didn't even know they were related until the big reveal.

I often imagine, if I knew I would meet or see someone for the first time, how would I prepare? Would I go shopping for something to wear to impress them? I'd certainly want them to meet those closest to me, my family and friends. Maybe I'd even jot down some questions or comments to make sure I don't forget the important stuff in our conversation.

Well, I'm curious if we are making preparations to meet Jesus? The Bible tells us in Matthew 24:42, *"Therefore keep watch, because you do not know on what day your Lord will come."* WE must be ready! Are we as anxious and moved by the thought of this reunion as we are those depicted of total strangers?

Adding to the Value of Others

Matthew 4:23 (KJV)

And Jesus went about all Galilee, teaching in their synagogues, preaching the gospel of the kingdom, and healing all kinds of sickness and all kinds of disease among the people.

What do people say when they think of you? Would they consider their life better because of you? Do you add value to them?

To succeed personally, you must try to help others. Zig Ziglar says, "You can get everything in life you want if you help enough people get what they want." So, how is this done? How can you shift the focus on others, adding value to them? Well, to start . . .

- Put others before yourself.
- Determine what they need.
- Meet their needs with excellence and generosity.

What A Deal

Romans 5:20 (NLT)

The law was brought in so that the trespass might increase. But where sin increased, grace increased all the more.

A recent advertisement read, "Free for first 30 days. It's easy. Just try it. After 30 days you will be billed $34.95 per month unless you cancel your order. Offer valid for 24 hours." I wonder how many actually fall for stuff like this? The product obviously isn't free! There's a cost after the first 30 days.

But, have I got a deal for you – GOD'S GRACE IS FREELY GIVEN TO ALL WHO PLACE THEIR FAITH IN HIM! For all time! Without God, we cannot earn – nor do we deserve – a reprieve from our sin penalty.

When we accept His gift, we are freed from punishment and enjoy sweet fellowship with God for all eternity. His mercy has no "fine print" and it's a deal we cannot afford to refuse, because there's nothing that can compare to it.

His Word Never Changes

Matthew 24:35 (NIV)

*Heaven and earth will pass away, but my
words will never pass away.*

Benjamin Franklin is quoted as saying, "In
this world nothing can be certain, except death
and taxes." While there is some truth to his
statement, it's not totally accurate. Rather it
would appear that cynicism is contagious.

A more accurate quote would be from
Albert Einstein who said: "God doesn't play
dice." While life seems uncertain in many
areas, one thing is sure. God is faithful and
He is true. His Word never changes. His long-
awaited Kingdom is coming, just like the
song we sing, "Your Kingdom shall reign
over all the earth." He is the Ancient of Days.
Because God is faithful to keep His promises,
our faith is never a gamble and our truth is
not blind. For the believer, the promise of
new life is more certain than the inevitability
of death.

His Kingdom will come and reign forever and ever. YOU CAN TAKE THAT TO THE BANK!

He Will

Psalm 23 (KJV)

The Lord is my shepherd; I shall not want. He maketh me to lie down in green pastures: he leadeth me beside the still waters . . .

Lyrics of the hymn, *Surely Goodness and Mercy*, say, "He restoreth my soul when I'm weary; He giveth me strength day by day." Psalm 23 is a reminder that we will all face trials at one time or another. Some of them are severe, like the death of a relationship. Loss. Illness. Devastating disappointment. Most likely something will come our way that is beyond anything we could comprehend. It's then that we find ourselves weary and worn. We seem to have more questions than we have answers, as we wait patiently on the Lord's direction. If we're not careful we will succumb to fear and anxiety.

It's in these uncertain times that we are vulnerable to the lies of our enemy. Yet, right in this moment, there is a truth that we can

cling to: GOD HAS NOT ABANDONED
US!

He provides a way station for the weary.
Our Heavenly Father is a dawn bringer –
overcoming dark nights. Jesus, of all people,
understands suffering and sorrow. He is our
source and our strength.

HE WILL RESCUE YOU!
HE WILL COVER YOU!
HE WILL RESTORE YOU!
If you're tired?
If you're weary?
COME TO JESUS!

God-Sized Challenge

Nehemiah 6:16 (NKJV)

And it happened, when all our enemies heard of it, and all the nations around us saw these things, that they were disheartened in their own eyes; for they perceived that this work was done by our God.

Before anything else, a leader must be COMMITTED! In this passage, Nehemiah was not only committed, but he brought it out in the others surrounding him, and the walls were completed in 52 days, despite their adversity. Nehemiah responded, "When all our enemies heard of it, and all the nations around us saw the things . . . they were very disheartened in their own eyes; for they perceived that this work was done by our God." WOW! What a great testimony! May this be the response of our onlookers in regards to our Kingdom efforts!

Leaders who complete a task possess these

four characteristics:

- *Compelling purpose*: They make a great commitment to a great cause.
- *Clear perspective*: They don't let fear cloud their view of the future.
- *Continual prayer*: They pray about everything and gain God's favor.
- *Courageous persistence*: They move ahead despite the odds.

Let me encourage you to cultivate these characteristics so that you will give the best opportunity for success.

Connect First

Exodus 19:3-6 (NKJV)

And Moses went up to God, and the Lord called to him from the mountain, saying, "Thus you shall say to the house of Jacob, and tell the children of Israel: 'You have seen what I did to the Egyptians, and how I bore you on eagles' wings and brought you to Myself. Now therefore, if you will indeed obey My voice and keep My covenant, then you shall be a special treasure to Me above all people; for all the earth is Mine. And you shall be to Me a kingdom of priests and a holy nation.'"

It's been said that before leaders touch a hand they touch a heart. Before God demanded His people keep His rules, He reminded them of His relationship and blessings. This was their incentive to keep their end of the bargain!

In this passage of Scripture, God spoke of

how He intended to bless Israel as His very own. He warned them of boundaries; then and only then, did He give them His commandments to obey. What a powerful example for us in leading others. Before He spoke His laws in Exodus, chapter 20, He took time to remind them of three important truths:

- The love He had for them.
- The victories He had won for them.
- The future He planned for them.

Before we, as leaders, make demands of people, have we earned the right to speak into their lives? I remember early on in ministry I read this quote at a church I frequented, "It's not enough to care . . . you must care enough." Shortly after I discovered that I sat next to a minister by the name of Zig Ziglar who said, "People don't care how much you know until they know how much you care." Enough said!

Grow to Your Potential

Ephesians 2:10 (KJV)

For we are his workmanship, created in Christ Jesus unto good works, which God hath before ordained that we should walk in them.

A plaque I was given early on in ministry says, "Your potential is God's gift to you, but what you do with it is your gift back to Him." Few people really dedicate themselves fully to their life's purpose. Instead they settle for much less than they were destined for.

Consider these four suggestions in growing toward your potential:

- Concentrate on one main goal. Don't become scattered in too many directions – FOCUS!
- Concentrate on continual improvement. This is key to reaching your potential.
- Forget the past. Jack Hayford, pastor of

Church on the Way in Van Nuys, California, said, "We can't gain any momentum moving toward tomorrow if we are dragging the past behind us. "Learn from your mistakes but move on.

- Focus on the future. You can become better tomorrow than you are today.

Being Before Doing

Proverbs 11:30 (CEV)

Live right, and you will eat from the life-giving tree. And if you act wisely, others will follow.

Some people think of leadership only in terms of action. But leadership is a lot more than that. Leadership is not just something you do; it's something you are.

While it's true that all leaders desire results, your "being" must precede your "doing." A common struggle often occurs when a leader's real identity and the desired results don't match up. But, when there is consistency in character, competence, and purpose, it makes a powerful statement to the people around them – and folks notice and desire to join in.

You've heard it said, "If you want to know if you're leading, look behind you to see if anyone's following . . . otherwise you're just out for a walk." If people are only following you because of your DOING, not your BEING, then you'll exhaust yourself trying to outdo your last big WOW!

If you want to do great things with your life, then seek to become a better person before desiring to become a better leader. Nothing great can be achieved alone. Any task worth doing requires the help of other people. And if you want to attract good people, you've got to become a better person yourself. If you're willing to do that, then you can leave the results to God.

Making the Tough Call

Acts 15:38 (NKJV)

*But Paul insisted that they should not take
with them the one who had departed from
them in Pamphylia, and had not gone with
them to the work.*

Perhaps the most difficult decision as a
leader is dealing with poor performers. If not
dealt with effectively, it will hurt:

- The organization's ability to achieve its
  purpose
- The morale of top performers
- The leader's own credibility
- The low performer's self-image and
  potential effectiveness

So, how's the best way to do this? The
leader asks, "Should this person be trained,
transferred, or terminated?" Obviously, the
answer will determine the appropriate course

or courses of action. By far the most difficult of the tough decisions leaders face concern terminating an employee, but terminating a poor performer benefits the organization and everyone in it.

Like a Rock

John 1:42 (NKJV)

Now when Jesus looked at him, He said, "You are Simon the son of Jonah. You shall be called Cephas" (which is translated, A Stone).

Dependability, in my opinion, is the most important characteristic for a team's success. It's important for the team to know who they can depend on and who isn't a team player. Here's a few ideas to consider:

1. Pure motives: If someone on the team places their agenda and themselves above what's best for the team, you might not label them as dependable. When it comes to team-work, motives do matter.

2. Responsibility: It's motivation that addresses why people are dependable, but it's responsibility that proves they are dependable.

3. Sound thinking: Dependability means more than just wanting to take responsibility. Desire must also be coupled with good

judgment to be a real value to the team.

4. Consistent contribution: If you can't depend on teammates all the time, then you can't really depend on them any of the time. Consistency takes a depth of character that enables people to follow through no matter how tired, distracted, or overwhelmed they are.

Fail Forward

Matthew 26:74-75 (BLB)

Then he began to curse and swear, saying, "I do not know the Man!" Immediately a rooster crowed. And Peter remembered the word of Jesus who said to him, "Before the rooster crows, you will deny Me three times." So he went out and wept bitterly.

It doesn't matter who you are or what you do, you will fail at some point. You've probably heard the saying, "To err is human, to forgive divine." That was written over 250 years ago by Alexander Pope, paraphrasing an ancient saying that was common during Roman times. In a devotional I have, there's "Rules for Being Human." Let me share:

Rule #1: You will learn lessons.
Rule #2: There are no mistakes – only lessons.
Rule #3: A lesson is repeated until it is

learned.

Rule #4: If you don't learn the easy lessons, they get harder.

Rule #5: You'll know you've learned a lesson when your actions change.

Norman Cousins said, "The essence of man is imperfection." Failure is simply a price to pay to achieve success. When we learn to accept this definition of failure, we can start moving ahead – and maybe even failing forward.

In Christ Alone I Place My Trust

Psalm 127:1 (NKJV)

Unless the Lord builds the house, They labor in vain who build it; Unless the Lord guards the city, the watchman stays awake in vain.

Security is found in the Lord, not in followers.

Unless God remains the focus of all that you do, your labor is in vain. Regardless of our profession, we can't fight, build, or plan well enough to gain permanence. Smart leaders don't add God to the equation, they put him front and center. It's only He who provides the strategy. It's only God who provides the security, so don't be looking for that from others. Let me share a list of rules to consider regarding security and people:

- People cannot provide permanent security.

- Leaderships should never put their emotional health in the hands of another person.
- Spiritual and emotional health requires the truth.
- Leaders must remember that hurting people usually hurt people.
- Troubles usually happen when leaders depend on people to do what only God can.

Be Good Followers First

1 Samuel 26:9 (NKJV)

But David said to Abishai, "Do not destroy him; for who can stretch out his hand against the Lord's anointed, and be guiltless."

Loyalty and trust are both key in leadership qualities. Leadership operates on the basis of trust. Before David became king, he showed respect for those who preceded him. Saul, however, didn't and lost his kingdom. Notice the vivid contrast between the two's leadership:

SAUL

- Self-conscious from the beginning
- Presumed the priestly office
- Disobeyed God in the little things
- Lost integrity by covering his sin
- Failed to submit to God-given authority
- Preoccupied with his own fame

DAVID

- Displayed God-confidence from the beginning
- Didn't assume any right or privilege
- Obeyed God in the little things
- Maintained integrity by respecting Saul
- Consistently submitted to authority
- Desired to increase God's reputation

With whom do you align, Saul or David? May we be men & women after the heart of God, pleasing to Him in all we say and do to advance the kingdom!

Careful or Careless Counsel

Psalm 1:1-3 (NKJV)

*Blessed is the man who walks not in the
counsel of the ungodly, nor stands in the path
of sinners, not sits in the seat of the scornful;
but his delight is in the law of the Lord, and in
His law he meditates day and night. He shall
be like a tree planted by the rivers of water,
that brings for its fruit in its season, whose
leaf also shall not whither; and whatever he
does shall prosper.*

The very first Psalm contrasts the right-eous and the wicked. The difference between them seems to be where they receive counsel! As leaders, we must guard against whom we allow to speak into our lives.

The first leader:

- Searches for wrong counsel

- Listens to wrong voices
- Joins the wrong inner circle

A second leader meditates on God's Word all day and the results are:

- Stability
- Inward nourishment and refreshing
- Fruitfulness and productivity
- Strength and durability
- Success

Team Works

John 15:13 (NKJV)

Greater love has no one than this, than to lay down one's life for his friends.

Someone once said, *"Teams that don't bond, can't build."* I know that's true in my ministry experiences throughout the years. If a team doesn't become a cohesive unit, they never realize the value they have together. When a team member cares about no one but himself, the whole team suffers.

The idea of TEAM was/is priority for me during my years in a local pastorate. So, the day of our mid-week service, my ministry team and I spent the entire afternoon preparing a meal for our entire church family. Imagine with me a bunch of novices shopping for ingredients and supplies, then actually cooking food for hundreds – it was an experience! We laughed, cried and solved more of the world's problems during those times. Thankfully, we had years to learn as we perfected our craft, because we served a very patient congregation. Team building concepts were learned in that setting that attending another conference or seminar would have never accomplished.

Also, our leadership team (a.k.a. board members) and their spouses met together, prayed together and served together. The idea behind this is that solders returned to the battlefield to rejoin their buddies because after you work and live with people, you soon realize that your survival depends on one another. TEAM is an absolute necessity in order to have effective ministry.

Vision Buy-In

Judges 6:12 (NKJV)

And the Angel of the Lord appeared to Gideon, and said to him, "The Lord is with you, you mighty man of valor!"

All leaders have vision. But not all people who have vision are leaders. Simply having a vision doesn't make someone a leader. And, a vision will not automatically happen. Followers must buy in to the vision of the leader.

Gideon had a vision to deliver Israel from its enemies, and the people had a choice to accept his leadership and his vision. Action was required, even though the vision was ordained of God. It also took time to process. Ultimately, so many people completely bought into Gideon's vision and leadership that God had to send a bunch of them home to make sure He got the glory for their victory. Be careful in leading and following that the glory goes to the right place.

Just because a person has vision and

occupies a position of leadership doesn't necessarily mean that people will follow. Before they get on board, they must buy in to the vision and the leader. It's not something that happens instantaneously; it's a process.

Leadership Questions

Psalm 137:1-6 (NKJV)

By the rivers of Babylon, there we sat down, yea, we wept when we remembered Zion . . . How shall we sing the Lord's songs in a foreign land? If I forget you, O Jerusalem, let my right hand forget its skill! If I do not remember you, let my tongue cling to the roof of my mouth – if I do not exalt Jerusalem above my chief joy.

The Jews were exiled to Babylon – no wonder they **cried!**

They couldn't forget Zion, the land of their birth – no wonder they **sang!**

They hoped and prayed for the day they'd return home – that's why they **dreamed!**

So, as a leader . . .

What is it you would you do if you didn't have to fear failure or rejection? ***What would*** *you dream about?*

Are there specific burdens that touch you and drive you to be more passionate? *What makes you cry?*

What causes you to rejoice? *What do you sing about?*

Higher Power

Psalm 9:10 (KJV)

And they that know thy name will put their trust in thee; For thou, Jehovah, hast not forsaken them that seek thee.

Mother Teresa once said, "I know God will not give me anything I can't handle. I just wish he didn't trust me so much."

Have you ever felt that way? There's no question that keeping the faith can be tough, especially during times of adversity. Exhaustion sets in, yet we can't sleep. God is silent, yet he expects us to rest in him.

It is at these critical crossroads that our faith is stretched. But if we will persevere, God will create in us a new level of spiritual strength. And we will understand more of who he is – and who we are in him.

Remember, you are a child of the King, the offspring of a sovereign heavenly Father. You have power from on high! Carry that confidence with you into this day.

Say What?

Ephesians 4:29 (NIV)

Do not let any unwholesome talk come out of your mouths, but only what is helpful for building others up according to their needs, that it may benefit those who listen.

God is a silent witness to each and every conversation we have. Every word we speak, even if it's in jest, anger, love or greed, He hears. Words that we speak that are uplifting to our family and friends, and those that are not, He hears. He hears words that bless, and He hears those that curse.

The example God provides for us in dealing with His children should be our guide. For example, He speak *with* us, not *to* us. He speaks lovingly to us, realizing we are weak. He never talks down to us or treats us according to our worst behavior. Even in his correction, our heavenly Father builds us up.

The Bible gives us a clear picture of the power of words as well. Psalms cheers us up;

Proverbs gives us wisdom; Romans points to repentance; Philippians exhorts; and Jude gently rebukes. I'm not sure what books or verses speak the most to you. Just remember, He is speaking and He is listening! So, my prayer is . . . "Lord, let me express myself in words that bless you and bless others."

Always Here

Luke 2:49 (ESV)

Why were you looking for me? Did you not know that I must be in my Father's house?

There are times along this journey that we feel abandoned and alone! We call out for help and God seems to be a million miles away. Our life takes unexpected turns and leads us down paths we never dreamed were possible. It's there in our questions that God will be found. He never leaves us alone – so don't be afraid!

Sometimes we worry and become anxious, wondering if God is truly watching over this mess. Things happen without explanation, causing concern, fear and even panic. Still, God is never apart from us. We are engraved in the palm of His hands. We are the apple of His eye. There's no need to run around looking for Him. Just sit quietly waiting for Him. He's always here.

Transformed

Titus 3:4 (ISV)

In grace our Savior God appeared, to make his love for mankind clear.

One of my all-time favorite hymns reads, ***"How marvelous! How wonderful! And my song shall ever be, how marvelous! How wonderful is my Savior's love for me!"***

In my recent travels across the pond, I visited some of the most spectacular places on the globe. I saw historic sites that blew my mind and viewed places that were only a concept in my imagination. Having been privileged enough to personally experience a few of the seven wonders of the world, like the Grand Canyon and Mount Everest, their grandeur left me speechless.

These places, they testify to the magnificence of our Creator. Still, the greatest work He ever performed is within each individual, transformed by His grace. God has taken our sin-sick souls, our messed-up lives, and made something beautiful. Through our heartache, He has carved out vast valleys with rivers flowing forth. He has revitalized desolate deserts of the soul, replanting them with lush gardens that continue to grow, through the help of the Holy Spirit who leads, guides, teaches, comforts and corrects us.

I am in awe of His wondrous works! I love Him!

Giving It Away

Revelation 4:8 (NIV)

Each of the four living creatures had six wings and was covered with eyes all around, even under its wings. Day and night they never stop saying: "Holy, holy, holy is the Lord God Almighty, who was, and is, and is to come."

A powerful chorus I remember singing as a teenager said, ***"We lift our hearts (& hands) before You as a token of our love."*** The Spirit of God would flood the sanctuary each and every time we sang it. ***"AS A TOKEN OF OUR LOVE"*** resonates in my spirit to this day!

I remember early on in ministry the Lord spoke to me to give away something that was special to me. I have to be honest with you – it was a real sacrifice to me! It was certainly against my human nature. Yet, I knew that surrendering my plans or possessions to benefit someone else – and as the song says to offer the desires of our heart for another's sake – shows our ultimate devotion.

Throughout Scripture, we are reminded that our hearts reveal our true character. When we give our heart to Christ, it not only speaks of our genuine dedication, but it results in a change of loyalty. Through our act of obedience, the Holy Spirit is then able to create within us a pure heart and spirit. God changes us and we can truly serve Him – renewed, restored, and transformed.

God is pleased when we give Him our all in love and devotion. I challenge you to think about a wholehearted commitment that will change your life and influence the people around you.

Imagine

2 Corinthians 5:8 (NIV)

We are confident, I say, and would prefer to be away from the body and at home with the Lord.

"Will I sing, 'Hallelujah'? Will I be able to speak at all?" These are lyrics from the powerful song, ***I Can Only Imagine***, by Mercy Me. I've heard this at a number of funerals and was privileged a few months ago to attend a private screening of the movie titled ***I Can Only Imagine*** which depicts the history behind the cherished song. It's powerful and I highly recommend it!

Songs have been sung, books written and even movies filmed in an attempt to understand the place called HEAVEN! The Bible gives us John's account of what heaven looks like in the book of Revelation, but even that is difficult to understand and comprehend. How can anyone describe a place that defies all human understanding and experience?

When we finally meet Jesus face-to-face, what will that be like?

We can only imagine how we will feel when we are standing before the King of all the Universe and our Savior. After all, He is the author and the finisher of our faith! I'm sure some folks will yell, "HALLELUJAH," while others remain speechless in His presence. I bet some will dance, while others bow at his feet.

If we've accepted Jesus as our Lord and Savior, one day we will meet Him face-to-face. We may have a difficult time imagining what it'll be like, but one day it will become a reality! And, it will be better than we can ever fathom.

Your Choice

Psalm 1:6 (KJV)

For the LORD watches over the way of the righteous, but the way of the wicked leads to destruction.

From before you were ever born, God loved you and chose you with purpose, provided for your every need, and comforted you in the most difficult of times. As our Father, He delights in doing this, just as we do with our children. Before I ever knew what my girls or grandchildren would be or look like, I loved them and made preparations.

God has a plan and reveals it in each step along life's journey. Still, because of God's great love toward us, He placed within us "CHOICE." We can choose to follow His path or another. He has also provided wisdom to choose wisely which path to take. He will never force His plans on us. From a Father who sincerely loves us, He desires to walk the path with us. Take His hand today and experience a new adventure! That's His desire, or you have the choice to WALK IT ALONE!

Sing

Ephesians 5:19 (NLT)

*Singing psalms and hymns and spiritual
songs among yourselves, and making
music to the Lord in your hearts.*

Why do you sing? I'm not talking about in
front of a crowd, so perhaps I should ask,
"What makes you sing?"

Martin Luther said, "When I can't pray, I
sing."

I love that! As you know, music & singing
are my love-language. When I don't find ade-
quate words to express myself, I can often find
it in the lyrics of a song.

I love waking to the sound of chirping birds
outside my window on those rare occasions.
But, scientists say that birds sing to make their
presence known; they don't sing simply for the
joy of it, but instead to signal other birds to stay
away from their partner or territory. It's
believed that each species has its own song that
distinguishes it from others.

What's your song?

Whatever it is, use it to bring glory to the Lord and to communicate to Him!

The Best Is Still to Come

Revelation 1:7 (KJV)

*Behold, he cometh with clouds; and
every eye shall see him, and they also
which pierced him: and all kindreds of
the earth shall wail because of him.
Even so, Amen.*

Perhaps you've heard the story of the woman who was diagnosed with an incurable disease and met to plan her funeral arrangements. After making the selections for songs, favorite Scripture verses and participants, the lady said, "There's one more thing, I want to be buried with a fork in my hand."

The minister asked, "Why a fork?"

She replied, "My mother always said to us while clearing the table to keep our forks because the best is still to come." She would be serving dessert next.

For a believer in Christ, the best-is-still-to-come. We will all come face-to-face one day with Jesus and it'll not get any better than that, so hang on to your spoon!

There's more to look forward to.

I'd Rather Have Jesus

Luke 21:3-4 (NIV)

"Truly I tell you," he said, "this poor widow has put in more than all the others. All these people gave their gifts out of their wealth; but she out of her poverty put in all she had to live on."

The old hymn says, ". . . than to be a king of a vast domain and be held in sin's dread sway. I'd rather have Jesus than anything this world affords today."

Many people believe that you can't be a Christian and have wealth or influence, given the statement in Scripture regarding the "camel & the eye of the needle." It's crazy to think that God would be more favorable of a person simply because of their affluence or lack thereof. I remember an event we provided at the church I pastored, bringing in a Steinway Piano Artist & members of the Symphony for a Christmas Concert. The room was filled with festive music and a celebration unlike any previous event. A great number of people attended who were season ticket holders of the Houston Symphony. They dressed in the latest fashions and were obviously blessed with means. At the conclusion of the evening, I provided a simple prayer and gave opportunity for those who needed Jesus as their Lord & Savior to pray with me. The next evening in a staff/board meeting, one guy said, "This is the first time I ever remember our church going after the 'up & outs' of our society." What a revelation.

Jesus is more concerned about what's in our hearts than what's in our homes/garages. Are we blessed with money, power and property that we are using to further God's work and His kingdom? Do our possessions serve us as we serve God?

Regardless whether we have little or much – what do we do with that which we've been entrusted? We should desire to allow the generosity of our great God to be seen through us.

Friend

Proverbs 18:24 (NIV)

One who has unreliable friends soon comes to ruin, but there is a friend who sticks closer than a brother.

Remember when we were kids and thought we needed to be friends with the popular crowd? We believed that by their association we would better fit in and have influence we lacked.

Do I have good news for you! You are friends with the Ruler of the Universe. He knows everything about you and even knows what your future holds. He is the only One who can guide you and sustain you. He is the friend that promises to never leave you, nor forsake you.

The great old hymn says it this way . . .

There's not a Friend like the lowly Jesus:
No, not one! no, not one!
None else could heal all our souls' diseases:

No, not one! no, not one!
    Jesus knows all about our struggles;
He will guide 'til the day is done:
    There's not a Friend like the lowly Jesus:
No, not one! no, not one!
    There's not an hour that He is not near us,
No, not one! no, not one!
    No night so dark, but His love can cheer us,
No, not one! no, not one

Clear Communication

John 16:29-30 (NKJV)

His disciples said to Him, "See now, You are speaking plainly, and using no figure of speech! Now we are sure that You know all things . . . By this we believe that you came forth from God!"

In a book titled *The 21 Indispensable Qualities of a Leader*, one chapter focuses specifically on clear communication as a leader. This is vital in every area of life, especially marriage, job and personal relationships. People are not prone to follow what they don't understand. They need to know what and where, how and when. You'll be a more effective leader if you follow four truths:

- Simplify your message: The key to effective communication is simplicity. Don't worry about impressing people, keep it simple!
- See the person: Ask, "Who is my audi-

ence?"; "What are their questions?" and "What needs to be accomplished?"

- Show the truth: Credibility precedes great communication. Believe in what you say. There is no greater credibility than conviction in action.
- Seek a response: Never forget the goal is action. Give the folks something to feel, something to remember, and something to do.

How well do you incorporate the four truths in your communication?

A Final Word

You can find Tim on the South Texas District website at www.stxag.org, on Facebook, or at his Houston office when he's not traveling his home state ministering in the churches across the South Texas District.

He'd be thrilled to connect with you and share stories of God's faithfulness.

Made in USA - Crawfordsville, IN
65377_9780578503103
02.05.2020 1420